The Boston Tea Party

A Narrative Poem
by Carole Charles
pictures by Bob Seible

THE CHILD'S WORLD ELGIN, ILLINOIS 60120

The Boston Tea Party took place on December 16, 1773, almost four years after the Boston Massacre (March, 1770) and over a year before the actual outbreak of the Revolutionary War (April 19, 1775).

In reaction to the Tea Party, Britain closed Boston's port, stripped the Massachusetts colony of all governing power, and prohibited town meetings. General Gage was sent to be the new governor, and he brought with him four regiments to enforce the new orders.

The closing of the port was devastating to Boston's businesses. But other colonies responded, sending or bringing supplies to Boston by land. Boston's citizens defied the ban on town meetings, and the elected Assembly defied an order to disband, merely locking the door against Gage's spokesman.

The lines of conflict were drawn. The Boston Tea Party foreshadowed the war to come.

Library of Congress Cataloging in Publication Data

Charles, Carole, 1943-
  The Boston Tea Party.

  (Stories of the Revolution)
  SUMMARY: Relates in verse the events of the
Boston Tea Party.
  1. Boston Tea Party, 1773—Juvenile poetry.
[1. Boston Tea Party, 1773—Poetry. 2. United
States—History—Revolution, 1775-1783—Poetry]
I. Seible, Bob. II. Title.
PZ8.3.C383Bo   811'.5'4   75-33156
ISBN 0-913778-18-4

Distributed by Childrens Press, 1224 West Van Buren Street, Chicago, Illinois 60607

The Boston Tea Party

Shhh, we must be quiet here,
Stay down low, and we'll creep very near.
Ma wouldn't like it if she knew,
But I must see what these men will do.

Haven't you heard what's going on?
Don't you know why the ships have not gone?
It's all because of British tea.
My pa's going to dump it in the sea!

Pa is in that group of men,
Each one is dressed like an Indian!
See the paint on each man's face?
They're going now. We'll have to race!

Where are we going? Down to the pier.
Remember the big ships anchored near?
They're British ships, stuffed with tea,
My pa said he'd dump some just for me.

We haven't had tea for ever so long,
Pa says it's because the tax is all wrong.

The patriots think it's their right to say
How much tax they should have to pay.

Here's a good spot, let's hide by this house.
Hush, now! Shhh! Be quiet as a mouse.
My pa would send me home so fast
If he knew I watched from first to last.

There go the Indians up the ramp!
I think that's pa, holding the lamp.
The navy's in the harbor; will sailors intervene?
I guess not. They're just watching the scene.

Now the Indians have the key to the hold.
All this excitement makes me cold!
Look! They're carrying the tea chests up;
This harbor will be a giant tea cup!

There goes the tea, over the side!
Oh, it's hard to remember to hide.
It's the biggest tea party Boston has had;
I'll bet it will make the Tories sad!

Look, they're sweeping off all the loose tea;
Soon that ship will be clean as can be.
No one was hurt, no damage was done.
Nobody even carried a gun.

Hurry! Let's duck! They're coming this way!
If my pa sees me, what will I say?
Uh, oh! Yes, pa, I've been watching you.
I wish I were older so I could help too!

Pa says the British will want us to pay;
They're angry about what happened today.
They might close the port and starve us all out.
Even I understand what this is about.

We're standing for what we think is right
And keeping our freedom always in sight.
We know we have the right to be free;
That's why my pa threw over the tea.